Matthew and Stephen

160201

Matthew and Stephen

(Mathieu trop court, François trop long)

Jean-Rock Gaudreault

translated by Linda Gaboriau

Playwrights Canada Press
Toronto • Canada

Playwrights Canada Press
The Canadian Drama Publisher
215 Spadina Avenue, Suite 230, Toronto, Ontario CANADA M5T 2C7
416-703-0013 fax 416-408-3402
orders@playwrightscanada.com • www.playwrightscanada.com

Financial support provided by the taxpayers of Canada and Ontario through the Canada
Council for the Arts and the Department of Canadian Heritage through the Book
Publishing Industry Development Programme, and the Ontario Arts Council.

The Canada Council for the Arts
Le Conseil des Arts du Canada

ONTARIO ARTS COUNCIL
CONSEIL DES ARTS DE L'ONTARIO

Front cover artwork by BraultDesign—Anne Guilleaume
Production Editor: JLArt

Library and Archives Canada Cataloguing in Publication

Gaudreault, Jean-Rock, 1972-
[Mathieu trop court, François trop long. English]
    Matthew and Stephen / Jean-Rock Gaudreault ; translated by
Linda Gaboriau.

Translation of: Mathieu trop court, Francois trop long.
ISBN 0-88754-764-8

    I. Gaboriau, Linda II. Title.

PS8563.A834M3813 2005   C842'.54   C2005-904162-5

First edition: July 2005.
Printed and bound by AGMV Marquis at Quebec, Canada.

This book is dedicated to everyone who helped create this play in French and English. And the journey continues…

By way of a preface

It has been a great privilege to have produced both *Mathieu trop court, François trop long* and its English-language version, *Matthew and Stephen*.

I'd like to thank Jean-Rock Gaudreault for having total confidence in me as a director, young as I was. Since then, we embarked on a journey that has now brought us to the creation of a third collaboration.

Above all, I thank him for considering and appealing to the sensibilities and discriminating intelligence children possess when he wrote this beautiful text. Of course, this is a play that is profoundly moving for adults, as well.

Matthew and Stephen has made thousands of children laugh and cry. We have performed the play 236 times in French and more than 30 times in English. Children have been completely engrossed by this wonderful story of friendship. A story about two small lives that intersect, about two vulnerable and fragile birds learning about trust and caring through play and the flights of their wild imaginations. They manage to overcome their fear of life… and death. The children in the audience meet these characters through a text shaded with a subtle sense of humour. They follow a compelling story that appeals to their ability to listen attentively, to the wisdom of their youth, and to the intelligence of their smiles and giggles.

And they show us, once again, how we underestimate their ability to be open and receptive, as long as we show them we really want to reach them! It *is* possible to tell children their own beautiful and complex stories, as well as our own. Their capacity for being observant and compassionate is incredible.

When I first read *Matthew and Stephen*, what attracted me to the script as a director was without a doubt the high stakes of this beautiful story. And of course, the quality and honesty of the writing that allows everyone to recognise something of themselves in the characters.

Jean-Rock's writing has a humourous tenderness that transcends the drama and existential questions of life like a sudden burst of laughter. Jean-Rock speaks the language of childhood—not children—a childhood we all carry within us. It's as if Jean-Rock is able to reveal the core of who we really are. So, here we are, big and small, excited that we are so alike, united by Matthew's and Stephen's adventure.

There is also a mixture of realism and poetry in the text that allows us to go beyond the anecdote. The taut rhythm of Jean-Rock's writing is a duel of short sentences, fired off with the precision of ping-pong balls.

And then there is the richness of his characters. The kind of characters that are always a joy for actors to perform. To truly play a child and make the audience forget the adult performing before them, to allow oneself to be amazed and moved, is perhaps one of the most wonderful and demanding challenges for an actor. Matthew and Stephen are both great, complex, and nuanced roles which are revealed layer by layer.

I truly hope that *Matthew and Stephen* will land on many stages, slipping under the skins of many actors, stirring the imagination of many directors and designers... because I know the joy there is to be had in discovering them.

As for me, my desire to continue working with Jean-Rock Gaudreault never ends. I want to go on bringing his true and beautiful characters to life. Because he makes me cry. Every time he sends me his words, he gets me... right in my heart! He always reminds me how we are all so fragile. How we are all so touching and funny... how we all want so much... how we all love so much.... He reminds me how open and wide-eyed we all can be...

Jacinthe Potvin
Artistic Director
Mathieu, François et les autres...

Production information

Mathieu trop court, François trop long, by Jean-Rock Gaudreault, created by Mathieu, François et les autres…, in co-production with the Théâtre Français du Centre National des Arts, and the Les Coups de Théâtre festival, was first presented at the National Arts Centre in Ottawa on February 24, 1998 with the following company:

Mathieu	Louis-Martin Despa
François	Gabriel Sabourin
Director	Jacinthe Potvin
Music composer	Catherine Gadouas
Set designer	Stéphane Roy
Costumes designer	Ginette Grenier
Lighting designer	Éric Champoux
Technical director	Carolyne Vachon

•

Matthew and Stephen, translated by Linda Gaboriau, was first presented using the same production as above, at the New Victory Theatre in New York on April 17, 2002 with the following cast:

Matthew	Daniel Brochu
Stephen	Eric Davis
Technical directors	Martin St-Gelais and Emmanuel Cognée

Characters

Matthew, 10-12 years old

Stephen, the same age

Matthew and Stephen

![1]

	STEPHEN comes charging out of his house, visibly furious. We hear his mother calling him.
STEPHEN	No, I won't go to that school! I didn't want to move, nobody asked my opinion! I don't know anyone around here!... Make new friends? It's too hard, it takes too long. *(He looks around.)* No mountains, no woods... just houses that all look the same. And papers on the ground everywhere. It doesn't smell of flowers, it smells of cars.... The sky is different, it's so low, looks like it's going to hit the chimneys. There's nowhere to pick raspberries, you have to buy them at the store. And besides, my room is smaller, much smaller. It smells of paint. We didn't take a vacation because of the move... I don't like it here. I don't want to grow up here. I want everything to be like it was before!
	STEPHEN walks away from the house, crying. Suddenly, a stone thrown from the house across the street falls at his feet. STEPHEN notices MATTHEW.
	Hey, did you throw that rock?
MATTHEW	It's a meteorite that fell from the sky.
STEPHEN	I know it was you.
MATTHEW	No.

STEPHEN	Why did you do that?
MATTHEW	Cause you're crying.
STEPHEN	I am not.
MATTHEW	C'mon, your cheeks are all wet.
STEPHEN	I've got a runny nose… I'm allergic to moving.
MATTHEW	Only babies cry.
STEPHEN	Throwing rocks is dangerous.
MATTHEW	It was just a tiny rock.
STEPHEN	You could've put my eye out.
MATTHEW	I aimed for the ground… since when do you have eyes on your feet? What are you doing on my street, anyway? I've never seen you before.
STEPHEN	I just moved here.
MATTHEW	Where do you live?
STEPHEN	The blue house.
MATTHEW	Not very pretty.
STEPHEN	Neither is yours.
MATTHEW	There are ghosts in that house.
STEPHEN	Ghosts?
MATTHEW	The man who lived there before used to kill all the dogs who walked on his lawn. It's full of the ghosts of dead dogs…
STEPHEN	Not true!
MATTHEW	At night they howl like wolves. They know how to unlock the doors and creep up the stairs without making a noise.
STEPHEN	An old lady lived there before us, and she only had a cat.

MATTHEW	Maybe, but the house is haunted anyway.
STEPHEN	How come you tell so many lies?
MATTHEW	I don't like new kids.
STEPHEN	I'm not a new kid. My family and I have been here for a week.
MATTHEW	(*trying to confuse him*) So, tell me… where's the corner store that sells purple licorice?
STEPHEN	Not far from here.
MATTHEW	That proves you're a new kid! There's no such thing as purple licorice.
STEPHEN	Yes, there is!
MATTHEW	If there is, it's poison.
STEPHEN	It's good, it tastes purple.
MATTHEW	Purple? That's not a taste, it's a colour.
STEPHEN	When it's orange, it tastes orange; when it's purple, it tastes purple.
MATTHEW	You're just a dumb new kid!
STEPHEN	You're the one who's dumb!
	STEPHEN crosses the streets and heads for MATTHEW's house. MATTHEW leaps up, picks up a stone and threatens to throw it at STEPHEN.
MATTHEW	Stay where you are! I don't want you coming on our property.
STEPHEN	I'm not on your property.
MATTHEW	Back up!
STEPHEN	The sidewalk belongs to everybody.
MATTHEW	That part of the sidewalk is ours, my uncle bought it.
STEPHEN	That's impossible.

MATTHEW	I'm warning you, I'm a good aim.
STEPHEN	Hey, stop it!
MATTHEW	Nobody's allowed to get near me.
STEPHEN	Who do you think you are?
MATTHEW	Everybody's afraid of me.
STEPHEN	I'm not.
MATTHEW	You should be.
STEPHEN	I'm much bigger than you.
MATTHEW	I don't like big kids.
STEPHEN	You don't like anything.
MATTHEW	I like being alone. I don't want people to talk to me. I want to be the only kid on the street. I want you to go back to where you came from!
STEPHEN	I sure wouldn't want to be like you.
MATTHEW	You don't know what I'm like.
STEPHEN	You don't have any friends.
MATTHEW	Either do you, you're too new. *(Silence.)*
STEPHEN	I'll make friends. I'll go to lots of birthday parties and have lots of fun. It will be almost like before, when I was happy.
MATTHEW	I won't let you.
STEPHEN	You can't stop me.
MATTHEW	I'll cast a spell on you.
STEPHEN	Go ahead, try.
MATTHEW	If you keep bugging me, I'll say the magic formula.
STEPHEN	There's no such thing as magic formulas.

MATTHEW	Oh, yes, there is. They're everywhere. (*MATTHEW picks up a popsicle wrapper lying on the ground.*) This is one, right here!
STEPHEN	It's just an old popsicle wrapper.
MATTHEW	That's what you think. (*MATTHEW starts to read the popsicle ingredients in a threatening, "magic" voice.*) Glucose, citric acid, guar gum, carrageenan, sodium benzoate…

> *STEPHEN runs around looking for a piece of paper to counterattack. He finds a roasted peanuts wrapper.*

STEPHEN	Barbecue peanuts!
MATTHEW	(*with a sneer*) Loser. Your "barbecue peanuts" can't ward off my evil formula. (*STEPHEN looks around for other papers.*) What do you think you're doing?
STEPHEN	We should find some more. We could make a book of spells, and figure out what they all do…
MATTHEW	You can't touch the papers on my street.
STEPHEN	I thought we were playing—
MATTHEW	Nobody plays with me. I bring bad luck.
STEPHEN	Nobody brings bad luck, not even black cats. Those are silly superstitions.
MATTHEW	The other kids won't talk to me.
STEPHEN	You must've hurt them.
MATTHEW	I didn't do anything to them.
STEPHEN	Then they're mean.
MATTHEW	Yes, they are mean. They call me the toad.
STEPHEN	You don't look like a toad.
MATTHEW	I've had chickenpox three times. It's a world record.
STEPHEN	What's your name?

MATTHEW	You tell me yours first.
STEPHEN	I asked you first.
MATTHEW	So what.
STEPHEN	My name is Stephen.
MATTHEW	Stephen what?
STEPHEN	Goodfellow.
MATTHEW	That's not a family name.
STEPHEN	It is so. My father and my uncle are both called Goodfellow.
MATTHEW	That doesn't prove a thing.
STEPHEN	Now it's your turn.
MATTHEW	My name's Matthew. Matthew Badboy.
STEPHEN	That's not your real family name.
MATTHEW	Why not, Goodfellow is just as stupid…
STEPHEN	We can't be friends if you don't tell me your real name.
MATTHEW	I don't want to be friends with you.
STEPHEN	Okay. Bye! (*He turns away.*)
MATTHEW	Baby! I'll tell you…. My name is Matthew Jackson.
STEPHEN	C'mon over to my house. We'll find a notebook for our magic formulas.
MATTHEW	I'm not allowed.
STEPHEN	Go ask your parents.
MATTHEW	My parents don't live here.
STEPHEN	That's not your house?
MATTHEW	No… but this is where I live right now.
STEPHEN	I don't get it.

MATTHEW	…my guardians.
STEPHEN	What does that mean?
MATTHEW	That they're responsible for me.
STEPHEN	Where are your parents?
MATTHEW	My mother is dead, and my father's away on a trip.
STEPHEN	I'm sorry.
MATTHEW	What are you sorry about?
STEPHEN	I'm just trying to be polite.
MATTHEW	Polite about what?
STEPHEN	My mother says we should apologise when we remind someone of something sad.
MATTHEW	What's your mother like?
STEPHEN	She's nice.
MATTHEW	You don't seem so sure.
STEPHEN	We just had a little fight.
MATTHEW	About what?
STEPHEN	Nothing.
MATTHEW	You don't want to tell me?
STEPHEN	It's personal.
MATTHEW	Okay. Everything I say is personal, so I guess I won't talk to you anymore. *(He turns away from STEPHEN.)*
STEPHEN	My mother says I'm not trying to make new friends. She's always in a bad mood these days.
MATTHEW	She probably feels guilty because you moved and you're finding it hard. So instead of consoling you, she's decided to be strict so you get used to it faster.
STEPHEN	How do you know all that?
MATTHEW	My aunt says I'm a clever monkey.

STEPHEN	Monkeys aren't clever.
MATTHEW	It's just an expression.
STEPHEN	I don't get it.
MATTHEW	Because you're just a child.
STEPHEN	So are you!
MATTHEW	No, I'm an old man.
STEPHEN	Oh yeah? How old are you?
MATTHEW	As old as I want.
STEPHEN	We can't choose our age.
MATTHEW	Yes, we can.
STEPHEN	If we could, there wouldn't be any children. Nobody would choose to be young, it's too long.
MATTHEW	I'm not talking about being older for real.
STEPHEN	So what's the use?
MATTHEW	Count to five.
STEPHEN	Why?
MATTHEW	Don't you know how?
STEPHEN	One, two, three, four, five…
MATTHEW	It takes about five seconds to count to five. But I know a trick. I concentrate really hard and I pretend each second is an hour. By the time I reach five, the sun has moved in the sky. One second can be a whole day, even a whole year…. That's how I can be whatever age I want. Sometimes I'm eighteen years old.
STEPHEN	It's just a game.
MATTHEW	A serious game. I've got a great imagination. My mother said so.
STEPHEN	I thought she was dead.

from the French production
left to right: Louis-Martin Despa and Gabriel Sabourin
photo by Laurence Labat

MATTHEW   She told me that before she died!

STEPHEN   Don't get mad. *(Silence.)* What's it like?

MATTHEW   What's what like?

STEPHEN   To be eighteen.

MATTHEW   It's fun. I've got a car.

STEPHEN   Where did you get the money?

MATTHEW   In my pocket. I've got magic pockets, in a big pair of patched-up pants my father left me.

STEPHEN   I can't believe you, no matter how hard I try.

MATTHEW   Tough luck.

STEPHEN   What year are you in?

MATTHEW   I don't know.

STEPHEN   You don't want to tell me?

MATTHEW	I don't go to school anymore.
STEPHEN	All kids have to go to school.
MATTHEW	Not me. I told you, everybody's afraid of me, even my teachers and the principal.
STEPHEN	But if you don't learn anything, what will you do later on?
MATTHEW	I'm going to be a professional sparrow-killer.
STEPHEN	That's not a job.
MATTHEW	I'm the best. Watch. See them over there on the telephone wire?
STEPHEN	Yeah.
MATTHEW	At least fifty of them.
STEPHEN	They look funny, all lined up like that. Back home, they never do that. (*MATTHEW throws a rock and kills a sparrow.*) Wow, you got it!
	When STEPHEN goes to examine the dead sparrow, he crosses the limit set by MATTHEW.
MATTHEW	Stay on the sidewalk!
STEPHEN	I just want to look at it.
MATTHEW	I don't want you in my yard.
STEPHEN	I've never seen a dead bird before.
MATTHEW	Stay where you are, you hear me?
STEPHEN	I thought we were friends…
MATTHEW	I told you, I'm sick! Really, really sick! My mother died of this sickness!
STEPHEN	You don't look sick.
MATTHEW	You can't see it, it's invisible.
STEPHEN	Is it contagious?

MATTHEW   It depends, it's complicated. Everybody's scared, they say, you have to be careful, sometimes, an accident, you never know…

STEPHEN   What have you got?

MATTHEW   I don't know the real name. But if I did, I wouldn't tell you because then your parents would never let you come over here, maybe they'd even want to move again, just because of me. I call it the sickness of our time, I heard that on TV.

STEPHEN   The sickness of our time?

MATTHEW   Yes, it eats the time you have left to live. Sometimes, I feel like I can hear it going tick-tock, tick-tock, like a watch…. The more time it eats, the sicker I get. At first, I was really scared, but everyone said you have to be brave, especially when you're a kid.

STEPHEN   Are you going to die?

MATTHEW   Apologise!

STEPHEN   Why?

MATTHEW   Because you said yourself that it's not polite to talk about that.

STEPHEN   I'm sorry.

MATTHEW   Everyone says I'm going to die, but I say I won't. I don't know how. I'm too young. Only old people know how to die…

STEPHEN   Two years ago, a girl in my class died in an accident.

MATTHEW   That's different—it was an accident, not a sickness.

STEPHEN   It's true. So maybe you shouldn't worry.

MATTHEW   You never know, maybe I'm wrong.

STEPHEN   I'm sure you're not going to die.

MATTHEW   You're just saying that so I'll be your friend, right?

STEPHEN   Yes.

MATTHEW	On one condition.
STEPHEN	What?
MATTHEW	You have to give me your best comic book.
STEPHEN	And what will you give me in exchange?
MATTHEW	Nothing.
STEPHEN	That's not fair.
MATTHEW	I'll let you come sit on my porch and you can look at the dead sparrow.
STEPHEN	*(after some consideration)* Okay.
MATTHEW	Bring it to me right away.
	STEPHEN goes home and returns shortly.
STEPHEN	It's a Zorro. *(Cautiously, he walks over and hands the comic book to MATTHEW. MATTHEW starts to read the comic while STEPHEN examines the dead bird.)* It looks like it's asleep.
MATTHEW	Birds don't sleep.
STEPHEN	Not even at night?
MATTHEW	Especially not at night. It's too dangerous.
STEPHEN	But they have to rest sometime.
MATTHEW	How can they lie down on a skinny little branch or on a wire?
STEPHEN	I think they sleep standing up.
MATTHEW	Impossible, they'd fall over.
STEPHEN	I know! They sleep when they're flying. When the wind blows hard enough, they spread their wings and glide through the air as long as possible. It's never very long, but if you add up all those little moments, it's long enough for them to get some rest.
MATTHEW	I can't read when there's noise.

STEPHEN   I can.

MATTHEW   Shhh!

> *MATTHEW resumes reading the comic. He bursts out laughing, then starts to choke.*

STEPHEN   Are you all right?

> *In lieu of an answer, MATTHEW throws him the comic book and hurries into his house, slamming the door behind him.*

2

> MATTHEW *is on his porch.* STEPHEN *comes out of his house and heads toward his friend. There's an old bicycle lying on the ground in* MATTHEW's *yard.*

STEPHEN   Hey, Matthew, hi! Where have you been, I haven't seen you all week.

MATTHEW   In hospital.

STEPHEN   You should have told me. I would've come to visit you.

MATTHEW   I didn't want you to.

STEPHEN   Did they cure you?

MATTHEW   No. I had the flu because of my sickness.

STEPHEN   You went to the hospital because of the flu?

MATTHEW   A bad flu with a fever, and bad dreams full of monsters. I hurt all over. I felt like an elephant sat on me. My flu is cured, but not my sickness.

STEPHEN   How did you catch it, it's not even cold out.

MATTHEW   I spent a whole night watching the birds, to see if they fell asleep.

STEPHEN   What did you see?

MATTHEW	I'm the one who fell asleep, with the window wide open. I swallowed the draughts of cold air.
STEPHEN	Is that your bike?
MATTHEW	I didn't buy it, I found it.
STEPHEN	I'll go get mine and we can go for a ride, okay?
MATTHEW	I can't go far from the house.
STEPHEN	Just once, we'll stay here on the street.
MATTHEW	If I pedal too fast, I see stars and I fall off my bike.
STEPHEN	We won't go fast.
MATTHEW	What's the point of riding your bike, if you have to stay on your own street and you can't go fast!
STEPHEN	Just a short ride.
MATTHEW	I said no! I don't ride my bike anymore, you hear me! It's too big for me anyway, it's for an adult. I just keep it so I can run away if my new medicine works. I'll pedal my bike from here to China, laughing and shouting all the way. You'll never be able to follow me. Nobody will.
STEPHEN	Sounds like a great trip. (*Silence.*) Do you take pills?
MATTHEW	Lots of them. At least ten a day. By the time I've swallowed them all, I don't feel like eating supper. I can't stand it anymore! (*MATTHEW goes into his house and reappears with several bottles filled with multi-coloured pills. He starts throwing pills into the street, as if they were rocks.*)
STEPHEN	Don't do that! They're supposed to cure you!
MATTHEW	They don't work. (*STEPHEN tries to gather up the pills.*) Leave them there! I want the cars to crush them. I don't want them growing in my stomach anymore, they make me sick, they're like seeds of sickness.

We hear the sound of a jet flying overhead.

STEPHEN	I hate that noise.
MATTHEW	It's just a plane.
STEPHEN	It reminds me of war.
MATTHEW	Weren't there any planes where you used to live?
STEPHEN	Sure there were. Lots of war planes, because there was a military base right near us. Sometimes they flew over the house at night. My mother always said they were the good guys.... But you can't tell, just by the noise. In the movies on TV, when there's a war, all the bombers take off at the same time. At night, when I was little, whenever I heard that noise, I'd get out of bed and, even when the planes were gone, I'd stay up listening.... It gave me a stomach ache.
MATTHEW	What did you hear?
STEPHEN	Nothing. But I stood guard. At the slightest sound of a nuclear missile, I would've run to warn my parents, so we could hide in the cellar.
MATTHEW	You don't even know what sound missiles make.
STEPHEN	They must sound like rockets. I was always afraid it would happen. I was scared I wouldn't be able to grow up. It was hard to go back to sleep.
MATTHEW	I wouldn't want to live there.
STEPHEN	When I got older, I didn't get so scared. I figured out that if the end of the world arrives in the year 2015, I'll still have time to do a lot of good in my life.... They say the sun is burning holes in the sky, that the icebergs at the North Pole are going to melt and the water will come up to our knees. They say there are huge meteorites silently passing close to the earth, and that too many children are being born all around the world.
MATTHEW	Some scientists will find a solution.
STEPHEN	But they're the ones who keep predicting all these disasters!

MATTHEW	I'm not scared. I always have to go to bed before the news.
STEPHEN	We should've been born a hundred years ago, before the world was so old. *(Silence.)*
MATTHEW	You got new shoes?
STEPHEN	For going back to school. I'm wearing them so they won't hurt my feet. I think I already have a blister.
MATTHEW	They look like soldiers' shoes.
STEPHEN	You think so?
MATTHEW	They're too shiny.
STEPHEN	I thought they were nice.
MATTHEW	I bet you're in no hurry to start school.
STEPHEN	I am, a bit.
MATTHEW	You're not normal.
STEPHEN	You learn lots of things.
MATTHEW	The teachers get mad all the time.
STEPHEN	Not if you do your homework.
MATTHEW	I know that school, they give you so much work you can never play outside after supper.
STEPHEN	But weekends you can.
MATTHEW	At school, they want you to grow up, but I'll never grow up.
STEPHEN	I'll ask my father to speak to the principal, so you can come back. He could get on the parents' committee…
MATTHEW	It's none of your business!
STEPHEN	But you'll get lonely, all by yourself.
MATTHEW	I've been absent too much, I've forgotten everything, they'd put me with the babies.

STEPHEN	I'd really like you to be in my class. I don't know anyone there.
MATTHEW	At least, if I was there, I could defend you. The big kids at school always bug the new kids. They make them eat sand.
STEPHEN	Aren't there any monitors?
MATTHEW	They do it when the monitors turn their backs. With those new shoes of yours, you're sure to attract the attention of Boynton and his gang.
STEPHEN	Who's that?
MATTHEW	Some stupid big kids.
STEPHEN	My old school was really cool. I knew everyone. I was captain of my grade's dodge ball team.
MATTHEW	At this school, they only play basketball.
STEPHEN	I don't know the rules to that game.
MATTHEW	You'll have to play skipping with the girls.
STEPHEN	Never!
MATTHEW	So just refuse to go.
STEPHEN	If only I could go back to where we used to live.
MATTHEW	My aunt has some bus tickets, I could get one for you.
STEPHEN	It's too far, it's in another town.
MATTHEW	It must be a lot prettier than here.
STEPHEN	That's for sure! Right behind our house there was a pond full of frogs and tadpoles, with lots of cattails.
MATTHEW	Cattails?
STEPHEN	They look like fuzzy hot dogs. I used to break off the fat end, and the down would fly into the air, like the fluff of a dandelion. It made me sneeze. My mother used to say I was allergic, because when I made myself

from the English production
left to right: Eric Davis and Daniel Brochu
photo by Laurence Labat

a white moustache with the fuzz from the cattails, my
lips would get all red and swollen.

MATTHEW I'd like to have a sweater made out of the down from
cattails.

STEPHEN It's warmer than sheep's wool. Cattails stay outside all
winter, but sheep have to go into the barn. You'd
never catch the flu with a sweater like that.

MATTHEW	Could you go swimming in your pond?
STEPHEN	No way! But sometimes I'd go for a swim behind my mother's back. She thought the water was dirty.
MATTHEW	How can water be dirty? We use it to wash ourselves.
STEPHEN	I know, but my mother…. If I could go back, just for a day, I'd bring you lots of cattails.
MATTHEW	You should divorce your parents.
STEPHEN	That's impossible.
MATTHEW	All you have to do is go to the police and tell them there's never anything to eat in your house.
STEPHEN	But that's not true.
MATTHEW	Don't you know how to lie?
STEPHEN	I can't leave my parents all alone. They don't have any other kids.
MATTHEW	They were alone before you decided to be born.
STEPHEN	They couldn't have been very happy, since they wanted to have me.
MATTHEW	Here come the sparrows…
STEPHEN	I'll try to kill one.
MATTHEW	You'll miss.
STEPHEN	Just watch.

> *STEPHEN picks up a rock and misses. He tries again, same result. A third time, in vain. MATTHEW throws a rock and kills a sparrow that falls off the wire. STEPHEN goes to examine the dead bird.*

It's all stiff.

MATTHEW	Don't touch it.
STEPHEN	I don't want to.

MATTHEW	I leave them for old man Johnson's cat.
STEPHEN	We shouldn't kill them, it's cruel.
MATTHEW	They'd die anyway.
STEPHEN	But they're pretty when they're alive.
MATTHEW	I don't think so. They're grey. If they were parrots, I wouldn't kill them. There's nothing tinier than a sparrow's brain. Sometimes they crash into our living room window.
STEPHEN	That's because they fall asleep in the air, that proves what I said.
MATTHEW	Flying's too much fun, I'm sure they don't want to fall asleep. I'd love to be able to fly. I deserve it more than them, with their little birdbrains. I don't know why they all come here. It's like they're making fun of me because I can't fly. (*He starts throwing rocks at the birds furiously.*) I'm a sickness for the birds, I prevent them from growing up and becoming parrots! (*One of the stones breaks the neighbour's window.*)
STEPHEN	Run, hide!
MATTHEW	Nobody's home. Those neighbours are always away on vacation. My uncle says they're rich.
STEPHEN	Maybe somebody saw us.
MATTHEW	Maybe.
STEPHEN	I've got a stomach ache.
MATTHEW	If the police come asking questions, I'll admit everything because I've got nothing to lose.
STEPHEN	Don't do that, please! Please!
MATTHEW	You can go to school in prison.
STEPHEN	Hey, you're the one who threw the rock!
MATTHEW	You didn't try to stop me.
STEPHEN	I never did anything wrong.

MATTHEW	You were my accomplice.
STEPHEN	I don't want to ruin my life!
MATTHEW	Don't cry, you big baby, I just said that to scare you.
STEPHEN	I wouldn't cry about that. (*STEPHEN dries his tears.*) My father says it's easy to go wrong. It just takes one mistake and you can end up in the street, without a job. (*Silence.*)
MATTHEW	I have to go inside now, my aunt and uncle will be home soon.
STEPHEN	They leave you alone?
MATTHEW	They have to, sometimes. Babysitters refuse to come to our house. It gives me a chance to play outside.
STEPHEN	Otherwise you can't?
MATTHEW	Not often. They're afraid I'll catch pneumonia.
STEPHEN	Pneumonia?
MATTHEW	It's worse than the flu. The flu is microscopic, but pneumonia's as big as a quarter.
STEPHEN	How do you catch it?
MATTHEW	Through your mouth. It's invisible and it's in the air. That's why you should put your hand over your mouth when you cough, so pneumonia can't sneak in.
STEPHEN	Is it bad to yawn?
MATTHEW	It's better not to.
STEPHEN	Could I catch pneumonia?
MATTHEW	Probably not. It's worse for people who already have a sickness.
STEPHEN	You're really unlucky.
MATTHEW	But I'm sure it won't catch me. (*Silence.*)

STEPHEN	I don't know if we'll see each other again before school starts.
MATTHEW	We'll never see each other again.
STEPHEN	How come?
MATTHEW	You'll make new friends.
STEPHEN	You think so?
MATTHEW	For sure. You won't want to see me anymore.
STEPHEN	That's not true.
MATTHEW	You'll be able to ride your bike with them, super fast and super far.
STEPHEN	I won't feel like riding my bike all the time.
MATTHEW	What are you going to do about your shoes?
STEPHEN	You're right. Now I don't know what to do.
MATTHEW	Give them to me, your mother will buy you better ones.
STEPHEN	I can't do that.
MATTHEW	Just say you lost them. I won't tell.
STEPHEN	My mother can always tell when I'm lying.
MATTHEW	I'll teach you how. Pretend I'm your mother…. Tell me you lost your shoes.
STEPHEN	I lost my shoes.
MATTHEW	It has to sound truer than that.
STEPHEN	I lost my shoes.
MATTHEW	*(playing an angry mother)* How can you lose your shoes when you're wearing them?!!
STEPHEN	Now what do I say?
MATTHEW	Think a bit.

STEPHEN	I was walking in the mud, my laces came untied, my shoes slipped off my feet and got stuck in the mud.
MATTHEW	(still playing the mother) Go get them, for heaven's sake!
STEPHEN	I can't. They're too deep. I'm afraid I'll sink in up to my neck. The mud's too dirty.... Do you believe me?
MATTHEW	Yes, but you have to break into tears and cry: "My beautiful new shoes…"
STEPHEN	I don't think it will work.
MATTHEW	It'll work.

STEPHEN rubs his shoes on the grass, and in doing so executes some funny gyrations. He takes his shoes off and hands them to MATTHEW.

You have to get your socks dirty.

STEPHEN	Right. (He rubs his socks on the grass.)
MATTHEW	You see how easy it is to become a criminal.
STEPHEN	Watch my bedroom window. If the light flashes on and off, it means my mother believed my lie.
MATTHEW	It's more my lie than yours.
STEPHEN	Maybe. But I'm the one who'll be punished if it doesn't work.
MATTHEW	What do you say?
STEPHEN	Thanks.
MATTHEW	Don't forget the light.

They both go home. Slowly dark. The light in STEPHEN's room flashes. Blackout.

3

> STEPHEN *arrives home from school. MATTHEW is sitting on his front steps.*

MATTHEW Stephen! Hey, Stephen!

> STEPHEN *notices MATTHEW. He looks toward his house to see if anyone is watching. MATTHEW senses his uneasiness. Guiltily, STEPHEN continues on his way.)*

STEPHEN Sorry, I don't have time.

MATTHEW What's the matter?

STEPHEN Not today. *(Silence.)*

MATTHEW You've made other friends, right? Is that it, Stephen? And they told you you should be afraid of me?

STEPHEN I have to put covers on my books.

MATTHEW What did they say to you, Stephen?

STEPHEN Nothing.

MATTHEW They talked about my sickness, didn't they? Did they tell you I was a toad?

STEPHEN I told them they were worms.

MATTHEW Who did you call worms?

STEPHEN Boynton and his gang.

MATTHEW	And you're still alive! What did they do to you?
STEPHEN	I told them you were my friend. They're so afraid of you, they left me alone.
MATTHEW	Wow!
STEPHEN	And when I've got the basketball, nobody dares take it—I told them you're the one who taught me how to play.
MATTHEW	That must be why they don't ride their bikes down this street anymore.

Silence. STEPHEN glances toward his house.

STEPHEN	One of the kids' mothers called my parents. Now they're scared. They won't let me see you anymore.
MATTHEW	Are you scared?
STEPHEN	No…
MATTHEW	Are you sure?
STEPHEN	I'm scared they'll get mad at me.
MATTHEW	It's like the colour of my eyes…. It's as hard as catching the colour of my eyes.
STEPHEN	I'm really sorry, Matthew. (*Silence.*)
MATTHEW	Last night, I heard a jet plane. I wanted a bomb to explode and destroy the sickness of our time. But then, I thought about how it would hurt you, too, and prevent you from growing up, and I didn't want it to happen anymore. I felt bad about wanting that.

STEPHEN goes into his house. MATTHEW tries not to cry. He is furious because he can't stop the tears running down his cheeks. STEPHEN sneaks out the back door of his house and comes to join MATTHEW.

STEPHEN	My mother's busy. But I can't stay long.
MATTHEW	Go away!

STEPHEN	I figured something out. Just saying it makes me scared. Because if it's true, I'll have to be careful all the time…. Grown-ups aren't always right.
MATTHEW	I knew that.
STEPHEN	That's 'cause you're a clever monkey.
MATTHEW	You said monkeys aren't clever.
STEPHEN	I thought about it again. You know how they imitate everything we do, except for one thing…
MATTHEW	What?
STEPHEN	They don't go to school. That's why they always look like they're laughing…
MATTHEW	*(bursting into tears)* It's true, that's true. *(He wipes his eyes.)*
STEPHEN	I didn't mean to make you sad.
MATTHEW	I know. It's not your fault. My mother warned me… she said I'd be all alone, that people wouldn't be nice to me… that I'd have to think about her really hard. But I'm tired of thinking, alone in my head. Too many thoughts…. You remember my trick with seconds?
STEPHEN	When you're eighteen years old?
MATTHEW	Yes. The other day, I counted to one hundred. I became very, very old. When I opened my eyes, all the trees on the street had grown really tall. Everyone had changed. But I was still alone, like now. The same! I'm a hundred years old, Stephen… because I don't have any friends.
STEPHEN	You've got me.
MATTHEW	Yeah, but you can't even come into my house. I have to stay on the porch, my aunt and uncle can't be around, your mother can't see us. It's like a prison.
STEPHEN	I'll try to talk to my parents again.
MATTHEW	They love you so much, they'll never say yes.

STEPHEN notices a dead bird.

STEPHEN   You killed another one?

MATTHEW   It's getting pretty hard. There aren't many left these days.

STEPHEN   Give them some bread crumbs.

MATTHEW   They won't touch them. They eat hours, minutes, seconds.

STEPHEN   I was thinking about your job as a professional sparrow-killer. I've got a better idea. One of my uncles has a big house in the country with lots of fields. In the spring, he sows seeds to grow nice yellow hay. My uncle has to chase away the birds. For them, the seeds taste as good as popcorn…. My uncle made a scarecrow with his old overalls, and rubber boots, a straw hat and an old winter coat. At first the birds are afraid of the scarecrow. They think it's my uncle guarding his field. Then, after a few days, they realise my uncle is much bigger than his skinny scarecrow. And they come back to eat the seeds… I thought you could be a professional scarecrow. You could throw stones at the birds that try to land…

MATTHEW   I'd have to stand out in the field all day. The minute I left to go to the toilet, the birds would come back. And at night, I'd be scared, all alone. And I'd get soaking wet in the rain. It's hard work.

STEPHEN   I thought you could try.

MATTHEW   Humans are the ones who are afraid of me. I could protect banks from robbers, prevent traffic jams, chase people out of theatres when the show's over. *(Silence.)* You know the woods behind the school?

STEPHEN   Behind the fence?

MATTHEW   Just on the edge, there's a pond. I think there are some frogs.

STEPHEN   If there are frogs, there must be cattails.

MATTHEW	You know what I'd like?
STEPHEN	I think I do.
MATTHEW	I'm going to leave you my entire collection of hockey cards.
STEPHEN	No, that's too much.
MATTHEW	You gave me your shoes.
STEPHEN	They were too shiny.
MATTHEW	No, they were really beautiful. My aunt got mad at me, trying to find out who gave them to me. I told her I found them in the mud…

       They laugh.

STEPHEN	We can make people believe anything we want.
MATTHEW	No, not anything. Sometimes even the truth is hard to believe. Your parents will go on being afraid…
STEPHEN	This is the first time I've ever known something no one else knows.
MATTHEW	What do you know?
STEPHEN	That you're just like everybody else, except you catch the flu more easily, you don't play baseball and you don't ride your bike.
MATTHEW	You forgot that I only eat pills for supper.
STEPHEN	I just saw my mother walk by the window. I better get going.
MATTHEW	Stay a bit longer.
STEPHEN	I can't. But I've got an idea—tomorrow's Saturday. I'll come out early. My parents will still be asleep. And so will your aunt and uncle.
MATTHEW	I'm scared.
STEPHEN	Of what?

MATTHEW	I don't know.
STEPHEN	Nothing can happen to you.
MATTHEW	I don't want to die.
STEPHEN	You don't know how.
MATTHEW	I'll fall down, with my eyes closed, like a sparrow. (*Silence.*) You promise you'll come over tomorrow morning?
STEPHEN	Promise.
MATTHEW	You better go, before your mother sees you.
STEPHEN	Don't be sad.
MATTHEW	I'm never sad! I'm the bravest boy in the world!

STEPHEN goes home. Blackout.

	4

Morning. STEPHEN appears with a notebook full of "cut-outs." MATTHEW comes out of his house, a blanket wrapped around his shoulders.

STEPHEN   Did you see the sun?

MATTHEW   What's so special about it?

STEPHEN   When it first rises in the morning, it looks young, like us. Are you cold?

MATTHEW   A bit.

STEPHEN   I don't want you to catch pneumonia.

MATTHEW   What's in your notebook?

STEPHEN   It's my book of magic spells. I found bunches of them in the kitchen cupboard. I cut them out.

MATTHEW   What for? We don't even know what they do.

STEPHEN   Maybe they could cure you.

MATTHEW   Or make me even sicker.

STEPHEN   I don't think they can be dangerous, or they wouldn't print them on boxes of food.

MATTHEW   Read them.

STEPHEN   Some of the words are really hard, but I practiced. *(in his magician's voice)* Maltodextrine… Lecithin…

	Papain… Riboflavin… Phosphate monocalcite… bacterial culture…. How do you feel?
MATTHEW	Sick to my stomach.
STEPHEN	They're not real magic formulas, right, Matthew?
MATTHEW	No, just ingredients. The whole world is made of ingredients. The houses, the trees, you, me. (*He looks inside his sweater, as if reading something written there.*) A child, pants, shoes, underwear, socks, sadness, dreams, memories… lots of memories.
STEPHEN	(*looking, in turn, inside his sweater*) Same for me. (*They laugh.*) Let's go swing in the park.
MATTHEW	(*shivering*) No, I'm too tired.
STEPHEN	Didn't you sleep?
MATTHEW	I'm tired anyway. But I know a game we can play sitting down.
STEPHEN	What?
MATTHEW	You wait for a car to go by and you guess who's driving it, where they're going, what they do in life.
STEPHEN	Not many cars go by this early.
MATTHEW	We can imagine them.
STEPHEN	That's even harder.
MATTHEW	No, it isn't. Look at that big blue one going by…. Did you see who was driving it?
STEPHEN	Who?
MATTHEW	My father.
STEPHEN	You remember how he looked?
MATTHEW	No, but I know it's him. He's on his way to the hospital to prevent me from dying.
STEPHEN	We're in the future?

from the French production
left to right: Gabriel Sabourin and Louis-Martin Despa
photo by Laurence Labat

MATTHEW	Yes. My father stole the recipe for the medicine that cures the sickness of our time. He left on a trip so he could save my life. Now he has to hurry. *(He stands up.)* Quick! Hurry! Hurry!
STEPHEN	If someone had discovered the cure, they'd announce it on TV.
MATTHEW	It's a mad scientist who discovered it.
STEPHEN	How do you make all that up?
MATTHEW	You think about what you want most in the whole world, and then you say it out loud. I hear another car coming, go ahead, try...
STEPHEN	It's a loud noise. It's a yellow school bus. The door's opening, the school principal's getting off. All the students are in the bus and they're watching us, their noses glued to the windows. The principal's waving at us to get on the bus. The kids convinced him you should come back to school. They all threatened to divorce their parents and their teachers if you didn't come back...

MATTHEW	That's another dream for me.
STEPHEN	That's what I want.
MATTHEW	But what would make you happy?
STEPHEN	To die of old age, even if it's in a nuclear bomb shelter, even if it's on a mountaintop stranded by a flood.
MATTHEW	There's another car coming. A beauty. Green. It just drove by.
STEPHEN	Did you have time to see inside?
MATTHEW	Yes. It was you.
STEPHEN	Me?
MATTHEW	Yes. I recognised you. You were much older, but I recognised you.
STEPHEN	What was I doing?
MATTHEW	You were remembering us spending this morning together.
STEPHEN	It must be hard to drive a car.
MATTHEW	There was a girl in the car.
STEPHEN	A girl?
MATTHEW	The girl you're going to love.
STEPHEN	Aw, c'mon…. You're just trying to embarrass me.
MATTHEW	No. There were even some kids. They were our age. Your kids…
STEPHEN	This is a strange game.
MATTHEW	I wish I could finish playing.
STEPHEN	Why do you say that?
MATTHEW	There are no more birds.
STEPHEN	Yes, look, there on the telephone pole.
MATTHEW	He's all alone.

STEPHEN	I think he's looking at us.
MATTHEW	I'm the one he's looking at.
STEPHEN	Hurry up, kill him, before he flies away.
MATTHEW	No need, he's going to die of hunger pretty soon.
STEPHEN	What can we play if you don't want to kill any more sparrows?
MATTHEW	Shhh, listen… (*Silence.*)
STEPHEN	I can't hear anything.
MATTHEW	The tick-tock.
STEPHEN	What tick-tock? (*We hear the sound of a very loud bird call. MATTHEW starts to cough violently and doubles over in pain.*) Matthew! Are you all right? (*MATTHEW is choking and shivering. STEPHEN runs to knock on the door.*) Matthew doesn't feel well! Open the door! Hurry! It's pneumonia! (*Blackout.*)

5

> STEPHEN *arrives home from school. He's happy.*
> *He is holding a bouquet of cattails. He goes to sit on*
> *MATTHEW's porch.*

STEPHEN Hey, Matthew, I brought you what you wanted...
I don't know if you've got enough to knit your
sweater. There are still lots of them. I think I saw you
drive by in a car a little while ago. *(Silence.)* Did you
notice how old the sun looks at this time of day?
I think it knows it's about to die. But it doesn't mind.
It can come back every morning. Lucky! *(STEPHEN
beats the porch with his cattails and breaks them. He
examines the fluff.)* I got my new pants dirty picking
them. I don't care, they itch. It's true that the water
where cattails grow is dirty. I'm going to tell my
mother I had to save a little girl who was drowning
in the pond, that the firefighters came and I'm going
to receive a medal in the mail. And if she sends me to
my room to punish me, it doesn't matter. I've got
time! I've got lots of time!

> *He stands up and goes home. After a brief moment,*
> *the light in his room flashes on and off, signalling that*
> *his lie worked. Blackout.*
>
> *The end.*

photo by Pierre Saint-Amand

About the author

Jean-Rock Gaudreault is a graduate of the National Theatre School of Canada's playwriting section. His first play, *La Raccourcie*, produced by Théâtre les Gens d'en bas in 1997, was remounted and performed during the Festival de Théâtre des Amériques in Montreal and was nominated for a Masque for best regional production in the same year.

His play for young audiences, *Mathieu trop court, François trop long* was nominated for a Masque for best script in 1999. Mathieu François et les autres… presented the play more than 250 times in Quebec and Europe. The English-language production, *Matthew and Stephen*, was produced in Canada and the United States in 2002.

His second play for young audiences, *Deux pas vers les étoiles*, first produced by Mathieu François et les autres… in 2002, has been performed almost 300 times in Quebec and France. It won the Rideau Vox Pares award and a Masque for best play for young audiences in 2003. Jean-Rock Gaudreault won the 2003 Governor General's Literary Award for *Deux pas vers les étoiles*, which was produced (in French) in Tokyo, in 2004.

About the translator

Linda Gaboriau is a Montreal-based dramaturg and literary translator. Born in Boston, Massachusetts, Gaboriau moved to Montreal, Quebec in 1963 to pursue education in French Language and Literature at McGill University.

She has worked as a freelance journalist for the CBC as well as the Montreal *Gazette*, and worked in Canadian and Quebecois theatre. Gaboriau has won awards for her translations of more than 70 plays and novels by Quebec writers, including many of the Quebec plays best known to English Canadian audiences.